Topics in Context

Context

Shakespeare – Not of an Age, But for All Time

Themenheft

Cornelsen

Context

Shakespeare – Not of an Age, But for All Time

Im Auftrag des Verlages herausgegeben von
Dr. Annette Leithner-Brauns, Dresden

Erarbeitet von
Martina Baasner, Berlin; Irene Bartscherer, Bonn; Lisa Braun, Meppen; Dr. Sabine Buchholz, Hürth; Wiebke Bettina Dietrich, Göttingen; Sylvia Loh, Esslingen; Benjamin Lorenz, Bensheim; Dr. Paul Maloney, Hildesheim; Dr. Pascal Ohlmann, Tholey; Birgit Ohmsieder, Berlin; Dr. Andreas Sedlatschek, Esslingen; Veronika Walther, Rudolstadt

In Zusammenarbeit mit der Englischredaktion
Dr. Marion Kiffe (Koordinierende Redakteurin), Dr. Christiane Kallenbach (Projektleitung), Aryane Beaudoin, Dr. Jan Dreßler, Hartmut Tschepe, Dr. Christian von Raumer, Freya Wurm *unter Mitwirkung von* Janan Barksdale, Irja Fröhling, Katrin Gütermann, Anne Müller, Neil Porter, Evelyn Sternad, Mai Weber

Beratende Mitwirkung
Ramin Azadian, Berlin; Heiko Benzin, Neustrelitz; Sabine Otto, Halle (Saale)

Layoutkonzept
Klein & Halm, Berlin

Layout und technische Umsetzung
Straive
designcollective, Berlin

Umschlaggestaltung
Rosendahl, Berlin

Lizenzmanagement
Britta Bensmann

Weitere Bestandteile des Lehrwerks
- *Schulbuch* (print und als E-Book)
- *E-Books* (in zwei Varianten: 1. alle *Topics in Context* bzw. 2. Schulbuch und *Topics in Context*)
- *Lehrkräftefassung des Schulbuchs* (im Unterrichtsmanager)
- *Handreichungen für den Unterricht* (print und im Unterrichtsmanager)
- *Workbook* (print)
- *Unterrichtsmanager*
- *Vorschläge zur Leistungsmessung* (digital)
- *Cornelsen Lernen App*

www.cornelsen.de

1. Auflage, 1. Druck 2022

Alle Drucke dieser Auflage sind inhaltlich unverändert und können im Unterricht nebeneinander verwendet werden.

Druck: H. Heenemann, Berlin

ISBN 978-3-06-036528-9

PEFC
PEFC/04-31-1156

PEFC zertifiziert
Dieses Produkt stammt aus nachhaltig bewirtschafteten Wäldern und kontrollierten Quellen.

www.pefc.de

Contents

Shakespeare – Not of an Age, But for All Time

*In many ways, Shakespeare's most famous *characters are still our contemporaries. Even people who have never read one of his plays know their names, their most famous *lines and something about the plays they appear in.*

Jules C.

party girl • secret wedding planner • tester of knock-out potion • Snow White impersonator

Verona

la_piccola@famiglia_capulet.[redacted]

Nørdman

studiosus philosophiae • theatre buff • overthinker • ghost whisperer • prince • serial monologist

Elsinore

H31@kronborg.castle.[redacted]

1 **a** Do some research on the *protagonists of the following plays by Shakespeare: *Hamlet* • *King Lear* • *Romeo and Juliet* • *Macbeth* • *Othello* • *The Merchant of Venice*.

b Read the social media profiles carefully and state which Shakespeare *character they refer to. (Refer back to the plays mentioned in task a.)

c You will probably have heard of some of the characters you identified in task b. Discuss what could be reasons that these characters are still widely known after more than 400 years.

2 From the words in blue boxes in the Chapter map, choose five. For each of the chosen words write one sentence about

- what it might tell you about this chapter
- how it relates to the guiding question.

Fortune's Fool

lovesick • party crasher • Cupid's target • balcony enthusiast • Mercutio's bro • hopeless romantic

Verona

figlio@della_casa_montague.[redacted]

Cruella MacThane

go-getter girl • supportive wife • dearest partner of greatness • sleepwalker • keeping up with the Royal Scots

Dunsinane, Scotland

cruella@dunsinane.castle.[redacted]

Rialto_Merchant

largest local lender • global trader • liquid capital holder • provider of favourable loan conditions

Venice

allthatglitters@venice.[redacted]

MacThane

battle axe • Highlander • kilt wearer • star warrior • dearest partner in greatness • follower of the dark arts

Dunsinane, Scotland

fergus@dunsinane.castle.[redacted]

Chapter map

immortal characters

adaptations

love

hate

language

Is Shakespeare still relevant today?

Chapter task: a Shakespeare adaptation

sonnets

theatre

power

Shakespeare's world

vengeance

The Shakespeare phenomenon

▸ More language

New ideas enter the stage

In the 16th and 17th centuries, Renaissance ideas coming from Italy widened people's intellectual horizons and challenged the traditional beliefs of the Middle Ages. Inventions and discoveries were made, explorers travelled the world and global trade expanded. The reawakened interest in the history, literature and mythology of Greek and Roman antiquity had a huge impact on Elizabethan society and culture. Earlier, mystery plays based on Bible stories had been performed by townspeople, or touring theatre companies had staged morality plays dealing with human virtues or sins. During Shakespeare's lifetime (1564–1616), drama developed faster than ever before. In London, theatres became thriving businesses, several new buildings were erected, and thousands of spectators regularly flocked to see the performances. Queen Elizabeth I (1558–1603) and her successor, James I (1603–1625), loved the theatre and supported several companies financially, of which Shakespeare's troupe became the leading company. New comedies, tragedies and history plays were written by Shakespeare and other *dramatists, such as Christopher Marlowe (1564–1593) or Thomas Kyd (1558–1594). The *plots of these plays were often not original inventions but borrowed from traditional stories or ancient sources and adapted by *playwrights.

▸ More info

The unknown Shakespeare

William Shakespeare, or the Bard of Avon, is widely regarded as the greatest writer in the English language. Little is known about the man, however. He was born in Stratford-upon-Avon, to where he also retired a wealthy man and died in 1616. He spent most of his professional life in London as an actor, writer of plays, and co-owner of his playing company. Since very little documentary evidence of his private life survives, there has been much speculation about his education, his beliefs and personal relationships, and even if he really wrote his plays. What endures of Shakespeare are not the facts of his life but his outstanding works, which are now an important part of world literature.

Shakespeare lives on

By the end of the 20th century, Shakespeare had become the most performed dramatist in the world. Many lines from his plays and poems are still widely known today, even if people are not always aware of where they come from. Some theatre companies have devoted their repertoire almost entirely to his plays and international Shakespeare festivals are held annually. The ongoing influence of his works is also shown by the many adaptations and spin-offs they have inspired in literature, films, music, the fine arts and pop culture down through the years. In every generation, scholars and literary critics have continued to analyse Shakespeare's texts and find new interpretations. Audiences and readers continue to relate to his *characters and their fates, demonstrating their timeless and universal nature. Some have become iconic, like Hamlet, whose line 'To be or not to be, that is the question' must be the most quoted line of any play. The tragic fate of Shakespeare's famous lovers, Romeo and Juliet, describes the outcome of a doomed love story, and Macbeth or Richard III embody the ambitious tragic hero or power-hungry villain. The Bard also contributed a great number of new words and memorable expressions to the English language that are still in use today: 'the naked truth', 'a shooting star' and 'the rest is silence' are just three examples. Shakespeare's continuing influence on our modern era makes him a genius well worth studying.

1 Words words words

a Find three phrases in the text that are new to you, two that you found interesting and one that you will always connect with Shakespeare.
b Note down an explanation of these phrases in your own words. Use a dictionary if necessary.
c In a group, present your explanations. The others guess which phrase you are referring to. Take turns. Add at least one phrase and its explanation from your partners to your list.

2 Word families

A good way to organize useful vocabulary is to create word families (words having a common base to which prefixes, suffixes or other words are added).
a Start a word family based on *write* including its phrasal verbs as well.
b Find three more words from the text and create word families with them.
c Choose three words from the families and write one sentence using each of them.

3 Chunk it!

a Replace the gaps in the following *chunks by verbs. You can check in the text for help, but also add other verbs. If you are not sure, use a dictionary.
1 '... people's intellectual horizons'
2 '... traditional beliefs'
3 '... inventions and discoveries'
4 '... a thriving business'
5 '... adaptations and spin-offs'
6 '... words and expressions to the English language'

► Getting started
► Check

b Compare your chunks with a partner and add new ones to your list.

4 Shakespeare wants you for drama

Inspired by a stimulating theatrical performance, you and your partner want to start an amateur theatre group at your school to stage Shakespeare plays in English.

You choose Work on either task **a** or **b**. Use expressions from the text.

a Create a poster inviting other student theatre enthusiasts to join your ensemble.

b **Speaking** Prepare an inspiring two-minute pitch for your project. Present your talk to the class.

► SF 42: Preparing and giving a speech, Student's book p. 324

5 A Shakespeare profile

Collect the documented evidence of Shakespeare's life and career and present it in a timeline. Add new material to your timeline while working on this chapter.

► SF 13: Doing research, Student's book p. 278

Understanding Shakespeare's language

Title page to the *First Folio*

- Explain the *images Shakespeare uses in the following sentences to describe the *characters' feelings.
  1 'Why, what's the matter, that you have such a February face, so full of frost, of storm, and cloudiness?' (*Much Ado About Nothing,* Act V, scene 4)
  2 'How sharper than a serpent's tooth it is to have a thankless child.' (*King Lear,* Act I, scene 4)

Info

Originally, **Shakespeare's plays** were not written for publication but only as *scripts for performances on stage. In 1623, after Shakespeare's death, his actor friends published most of his plays in the *First Folio* edition and divided them into three categories: comedies, tragedies and history plays.
Tragedies focus on a single high-ranking *character, the tragic hero, who contributes to or is driven to his death by his own weakness in character (tragic flaw) in the final *act, a fate which appeals to the audience's sympathy or pity. Usually, not only the *protagonist's own life but the whole state is thrown into disorder, e.g. by the murder of a king. Order must then be restored, e.g. by the installation of the rightful heir to the throne.

This short passage from Shakespeare's tragedy Macbeth, *in which the *protagonist reacts to the news of his wife's death, gives an impression of the type of *verse that is typical of Shakespeare's plays.*

MACBETH Tomorrow, and tomorrow, and tomorrow,
Creeps in this petty pace from day to day
To the last syllable of recorded time,
And all our yesterdays have lighted fools
The way to dusty death. Out, out, brief candle!
Life's but a walking shadow, a poor player
That struts and frets his hour upon the stage
And then is heard no more: it is a tale
Told by an idiot, full of sound and fury,
Signifying nothing.

From: Macbeth, *Act V, scene 5*

Annotations
1 **and tomorrow** or the next day
2 **in this petty pace** slowly
3 **to the last syllable of recorded time** until the end of time
4 **our yesterdays** the days gone by, the past
4 **light** *(v)* show
5 **brief** short
6 **walking shadow** actor, illusion
6 **poor** bad
7 **strut** *(v)* walk proudly
7 **fret** *(v)* worry
7 **his hour** when he is performing
9 **sound and fury** noise and anger
10 **signify** mean

Comprehension

1 Rewrite what Macbeth says in modern English prose.

Analysis

2 Analyse the *imagery used in this speech and examine its effect on the reader.

Language awareness

Info

Shakespeare wrote mostly in **blank verse**, i.e. regular *metrical but unrhymed lines. The *rhythm was usually **iambic** [aɪˈæmbɪk] **pentameter**, i.e. ten syllables with five stressed syllables to a line with the stress on dum: di dum, di dum, di dum, di dum, di dum. When using prose, Shakespeare often changed the *intonation or pronunciation of words (e.g. stressing the ending -èd) to make it more suitable to *verse.

To avoid monotony, Shakespeare varies his meter by using eleven syllables or by running one line into the next ('enjambement' or 'run-on line'); he creates pauses in the middle of a line or divides a line between two speakers. The meter also varies when *characters are experiencing strong emotions. Occasionally, he uses meters of four, six or eight beats, e.g. for songs or the magic spells of the three witches in *Macbeth*:

> 'Double, double, toil and trouble,
> Fire burn and cauldron bubble.' (IV, 1)

To express a character's emotions, often at the end of a *scene, Shakespeare uses rhyming *couplets, e.g. when Hamlet (in the play that bears his name) feels uneasy about having to avenge his father's death:

> 'The time is out of joint: O cursèd spite,
> That ever I was born to set it right.' (I, 5)

3 **a** First, read out the prose version that you wrote in task **1**; then, read Shakespeare's verses aloud applying the information about the iambic pentameter from the info box.

b Compare the effect of the two versions on the listeners. Also explain what difference it makes to the speaker, e.g. if they have to learn the text by heart.

▶ More language

Beyond the text

4 Shakespeare has contributed numerous words and phrases to the English language.

a Choose one of the phrases below and explain what it means. You may look it up online if you need help.

- 'What's done is done' (*Macbeth,* Act II, scene 3)
- 'All that glisters is not gold' (*The Merchant of Venice,* Act II, scene 7)
- 'Greek to me' (*Julius Caesar,* Act I, scene 2)
- 'A fool's paradise' (*Romeo and Juliet,* Act II, scene 3)
- 'I must be cruel, only to be kind' (*Hamlet,* Act III, scene 4)
- 'Though this be madness, yet there is method in't' (*Hamlet,* Act III, scene 2)
- 'The world's mine oyster' (*The Merry Wives of Windsor,* Act II, scene 2)
- 'Spotless reputation' (*Richard II,* Act I, scene 1)

b Speaking Work on one of the tasks below:

- In groups, write a short *dialogue that contains at least three different phrases from **4a**, rehearse it and present it to the class.
- Challenge In groups, write a short *dialogue in blank verse that contains at least three different phrases from **4a**, rehearse it and present it to the class.

Text 2

Annotations

1 **O for** if only we had
1 **Muse of fire** divine inspiration
1 **ascend** rise, climb
2 **invention** creative imagination
4 **behold** look at, see
4 **swelling** majestic
5 **warlike** ready to fight
5 **Harry** King Henry V
6 **assume the port of Mars** appear like the Roman god of war
7 **leashed in** not yet let loose
7 **hound** *(n)* hunting dog
7 **famine** severe lack of food that threatens people's lives
8 **crouch for employment** wait for their attack
8 **gentles** ladies and gentlemen
9 **flat unraisèd spirits** dull, ordinary actors
10 **scaffold** stage
11 **cockpit** theatrical arena
13 **wooden O** synonym for the circular theatre
13 **the very casques** the real helmets
14 **affright sb.** frighten sb.
14 **Agincourt** place in Northern France where the English army won an important battle against the French in 1415
15 **crookèd figure** the number zero
16 **attest in little place a million** can turn a low number into a million
17 **ciphers** zeros, noughts; here: actors
17 **accompt** account, judgement

The stage is all the world

- Explain why a theatrical performance has a different effect on the audience than merely reading the play.

Info

Shakespeare's **history plays** deal with British kings' lives and deaths and usually feature battles, coronations, funerals, etc. He focused more on dramatic effect than on historical accuracy and intended to show what qualities a king should possess to deal with domestic opponents, as well as enemies abroad.

In the prologue at the beginning of Shakespeare's history play Henry V, *the play's chorus (a group of actors who comment on the play's action and narrate events that are not performed on stage) reflects on how important the powers of imagination are for a theatrical performance.*

CHORUS O for a Muse of fire, that would ascend
The brightest heaven of invention,
A kingdom for a stage, princes to act
And monarchs to behold the swelling scene!
Then should the warlike Harry, like himself,
Assume the port of Mars; and at his heels,
Leashed in like hounds, should famine, sword and fire
Crouch for employment. But pardon, and gentles all,
The flat unraisèd spirits that have dared
On this unworthy scaffold to bring forth
So great an object: can this cockpit hold
The vasty fields of France? Or may we cram
Within this wooden O the very casques
That did affright the air at Agincourt?
O, pardon! Since a crookèd figure may
Attest in little place a million;
And let us, ciphers to this great accompt,
On your imaginary forces work. [...]

From: Henry V, *Act I, Prologue*

Comprehension

1 Complete the following sentences using information from the excerpt you just read.
1 Although it is just a small space, a stage can contain ...
2 Even though actors are common people, they can ...
3 In the world of theatre, everything is made possible by ...

Analysis

2 You choose Work on either task **a** or **b**.

a Examine the *imagery used in the text and the effect created by it.

b Analyse the way the chorus addresses the audience and the effect this may have on their experience of the performance they are about to see.

Language awareness

3 **a** Find examples in the text where Shakespeare uses the same syntactical structures repeatedly to build his sentences.
b Rewrite them in a way that avoids repetitions.
c Compare the two versions and analyse the effect of repeating a particular sentence structure on the reader or listener.

Beyond the text

Info

From the mid-sixteenth century onwards, several professional theatre companies performed in London. The first commercial theatre opened in 1576, and Shakespeare's company, 'The Lord Chamberlain's Men', built the first **Globe theatre,** the 'Wooden O', in 1599. The city council had banned the companies from playing within the city limits, so they built their theatres across the river Thames, in Southwark. In 1997, a modern reconstruction of the Globe opened, only 200 yards from the original site.

4 **a** Do some research to find out more about the Globe and other theatres in Shakespeare's time. Focus on the following questions:
- How were the theatres managed and financed?
- What did the interior look like?
- What was the atmosphere like and how did the audience respond to the performance?

b Discuss how the external conditions of the theatre performances may have influenced the plays Shakespeare wrote and the way they were performed.

Historical sketch of The Swan, a London theatre built in 1594

▸ Getting started

Shakespeare and his time

Info

During Shakespeare's lifetime, England was ruled by **Queen Elizabeth I**, who reigned from 1558 to 1603. Since she never married, the crown passed to her cousin James VI, the king of Scotland, whose troubled reign lasted from 1603 to 1625.

Portrait of Elizabeth I (1592)

Elizabeth's father Henry VIII had founded the **Anglican Church** and made Protestantism the state religion, which led to bitter conflicts with the Roman Catholic Church and unsuccessful attempts by Spain to overthrow Elizabeth. Despite some domestic rebellions by sections of the aristocracy, the queen's 45-year-long reign was an era of relative stability and prosperity, in which especially trade, exploration and literature, like drama, flourished.

Several concepts dating from the Middle Ages still governed the **Elizabethan worldview**, despite the spread of Renaissance ideas and the widening of people's horizons. According to the concept of **The Chain of Being,** each living and lifeless thing had a fixed place in a divine ranking system, which in order to prevent chaos must never be upset. People also believed in the power of fate, or **Fortune**, and saw a direct link between the order of the universe and the life of human beings on earth, who they thought were strongly influenced by what happened in the cosmos (Macrocosm > Microcosm).

Like all other creatures, man was also believed to be made of the four elements fire, air, water and earth, which in the form of bodily fluids known as the **Four Humours** ruled the person. In Shakespeare's works, there are many references to these notions, and his *characters' actions and convictions are based on this set of beliefs.

Annotations
Prime first hour of daylight, when a prayer should be said
Galen important ancient physician of the 2nd century AD
empiric medical practitioner without a degree from medical college

▸ Getting started

You are going to listen to an excerpt from Cassidy Cash's podcast That Shakespeare Life. *Cash talks to Professor Barbara Traister, who teaches medical history at university, about the role of astrology in medicine in Shakespeare's time.*

Comprehension

1 Listening Complete the following sentences.

1 In the Elizabethan era, doctors would use astrology to ....
2 The concept of the Four Humours originates from ...
3 According to this concept, a person is healthy if ...
4 If you were a melancholy person, i.e. had too much black bile, you might ...
5 Astrology was important for understanding the distribution of the fluids in a person's body because ...
6 Physicians would often draw a horoscope because ...
7 When Shakespeare referred to the Four Humours in his plays, his audience would ...

Beyond the text

2 If we believed, like Shakespeare and his audience did, that the course of a person's life was influenced by fate and the constellations of the planets – would we judge his *characters and their actions differently? Discuss the question.

3 In groups, find out more about different aspects of political and social life in Shakespeare's time:

- social structure
- women's lives
- exploration and trade
- Shakespeare's London
- amusements and pastimes
- crime and punishment
- witchcraft, magic and religion.

►SF 13: Doing research, Student's book p. 278

a Each group chooses one topic, and all group members, who are the experts on this topic, write down the results.

b Then, new groups are formed with one member of each expert group, who present their findings to the others. All group members take notes on the topics the other members have worked on.

Work on either task **c** or **d**.

c All students go back to their original groups and share the information they gathered.

d **Challenge** All students go back to their original groups and share the information they gathered. In your group, create a podcast or a short video on the topic you worked on.

Text 4

The seven ages of man

- Speculate on what your life might look like in your thirties, forties, fifties, sixties, seventies, eighties, etc.

► Getting started

Info

Shakespeare's comedies usually deal with romantic relationships that are complicated by misunderstandings, quarrels or the involvement of others who intend to keep the two lovers apart, but which end happily, very often with marriage. Apart from surprising *plot twists or even improbable events, the plays contain comic *characters who often add a light-hearted mood. Devices such as disguises, mistaken identities, witty exchanges and a quick pace of *action are characteristic features. Villains are usually stopped just in time and virtue wins over vice.

In the comedy As You Like It, *Shakespeare has one of his characters, Jaques* [jæ'kwəz], *reflect on the different stages of our lives.*

All the world's a stage,
And all the men and women merely players:
They have their exits and their entrances;
And one man in his time plays many parts,
His acts being seven ages. At first the infant,
Mewling and puking in the nurse's arms.

Annotations
2 **merely** only
4 **part** *(n)* role
5 **act** *(n)* role
5 **infant** small child
6 **mewl** cry
6 **puke** throw up

Annotations
7 **whine** complain
7 **satchel** schoolbag
10 **furnace** oven for heating metal to very high temperatures
10 **woeful ballad** sad song
12 **full of strange oaths** foul-mouthed
12 **pard** leopard
13 **jealous in honour** quickly insulted
13 **quick in quarrel** quick to start a fight
14 **seek sth.** look for sth., try to achieve sth.
14 **bubble reputation** illusion of brief fame
15 **justice** judge
16 **capon** fattened chicken
17 **with eyes severe** looking grim
17 **formal** regular
18 **wise saws** moral sayings
18 **modern instances** banal, well known arguments
19 **shift** *(v)* move
20 **lean** thin
20 **pantaloon** silly old man
21 **pouch** purse
22 **hose** stockings
22 **well saved** carefully stored up
23 **shrunk shank** thin leg
24 **treble** high-pitched voice
26 **strange eventful history** wonderful play rich in incidents
27 **mere oblivion** total forgetfulness
28 **sans** *(French)* without

And then the whining schoolboy, with his satchel
And shining morning face, creeping like snail
Unwillingly to school. And then the lover,
Sighing like furnace, with a woeful ballad
Made to his mistress' eyebrow. Then a soldier,
Full of strange oaths, and bearded like the pard,
Jealous in honour, sudden, and quick in quarrel,
Seeking the bubble reputation
Even in the cannon's mouth. And then the justice,
In fair round belly with good capon lined,
With eyes severe and beard of formal cut,
Full of wise saws and modern instances;
And so he plays his part. The sixth age shifts
Into the lean and slippered pantaloon,
With spectacles on nose, and pouch on side,
His youthful hose, well saved, a world too wide
For his shrunk shank, and his big manly voice,
Turning again toward childish treble, pipes
And whistles in his sound. Last scene of all,
That ends this strange eventful history,
Is second childishness, and mere oblivion,
Sans teeth, sans eyes, sans taste, sans everything.

From: As You Like It, *Act II, scene 7*

Comprehension

1 **a** State what life is compared to in the first five lines.
b Sum up briefly what Jaques says about the seven ages of man.

Analysis

2 Analyse the *images Shakespeare uses to describe man's progress through the seven ages of his life.

3 Viewing Watch the animation of the speech from the TED-Ed series *There's a Poem for That*. Analyse the visual devices used in the animation and state how suitable you find them.

Language awareness

4 **a** Find all expressions in the text that specifically refer to a boy or a man.
b Try to replace them with a female equivalent.
c Compare the effect of the two versions on the reader. Do you think that 'all the men and women' (l. 2) can relate to Shakespeare's description of the seven ages in the same way?

Beyond the text

5 Analyse the *cartoon below. Compare its representation of the nine ages to the way Shakespeare describes man's seven ages. ► Language help

6 Outline other ways in which the stages of life could be illustrated.

►SF 23: Analysing cartoons, Student's book p. 293

Language help

be pushed in ... • pram • wheelchair • tricycle • motorhome • mobility scooter

Our little life is rounded with a sleep

- With a partner discuss how you'd like to be remembered by people you love.

Shakespeare was a great explorer of the human soul. Often, he holds the mirror to people's all too grand self-images and their desire for immortal fame. In his 'Sonnet 71' (1609), he reflects on whether there is any sense in keeping loved ones who have died in our memories. Reflecting on the same question, Christina Rossetti (1830–1894) takes a different perspective in her poem 'Remember' (1849).

Sonnet 71 William Shakespeare

No longer mourn for me when I am dead
Than you shall hear the surly sullen bell
Give warning to the world that I am fled
From this vile world with vilest worms to dwell;
Nay, if you read this line, remember not
The hand that writ it; for I love you so,
That I in your sweet thoughts would be forgot,
If thinking on me then should make you woe.
O, if I say you look upon this verse,
When I perhaps compounded am with clay,
Do not so much as my poor name rehearse,
But let your love even with my life decay,
Lest the wise world should look into your moan,
And mock you with me after I am gone.

► More info

Annotations

1 **No longer mourn for me when I am dead than** do not let your sad feelings about my death last longer than
2 **surly sullen bell** gloomy funeral bell
4 **vile** evil
4 **dwell** stay
6 **writ** wrote
7 **would be** want to be
8 **make you woe** cause you to mourn
10 **compounded** mixed
10 **clay** heavy, sticky earth used to make pots
11 **rehearse** repeat
12 **decay** die
13 **lest** for fear that
13 **the wise world** the world in its wisdom
13 **look into your moan** want to find out about your sorrow
14 **mock you with me** mock you because of me

Text 5

Annotations
- **8 counsel** *(v)* listen to and advise
- **10 grieve** mourn
- **12 vestige of sth.** ['vestɪdʒ] small part of sth. that still exists

Remember Christina Rossetti

Remember me when I am gone away,
Gone far away into the silent land;

When you can no more hold me by the hand,
Nor I half turn to go yet turning stay.
Remember me when no more day by day
You tell me of our future that you planned:
Only remember me; you understand
It will be late to counsel then or pray.
Yet if you should forget me for a while
And afterwards remember, do not grieve:
For if the darkness and corruption leave
A vestige of the thoughts that once I had,
Better by far you should forget and smile
Than that you should remember and be sad.

Comprehension

1 a Sum up the main ideas of the two sonnets.
b State who is speaking to whom in both poems and what is the intention of each poem's *speaker.

Analysis

2 Analyse the mood of both sonnets and point out where a change of mind can be found in the *speakers' statements.

Language awareness

3 a Examine the choice of words and the *images both *speakers use to describe death. Would you use them if you had to write a letter of condolence? Explain why, or why not.
b Find more expressions suitable for this purpose.

Beyond the text

4 You choose | Writing Work on either task **a** or **b**.
a Choose one sonnet and rewrite it in modern English in the form of a poem or a song. Use some of the expressions that you collected in tasks **3 a** and **b**.
b Imagine you are the addressee of one of the sonnets. Write a letter replying to its speaker. Use some of the expressions that you collected in tasks **3 a** and **b**.

►SF 36: Creative writing, Student's book p. 311
►SF 33: Writing a formal letter, Student's book p. 307

5 *Sonnet 71* has been frequently chosen for poetry collections, and *Remember Me*, a choral song version of Rossetti's poem composed by Bob Chilcott, is often performed. Assess why both sonnets are still popular.

Vengeance is in my heart

- What negative consequences could happen if people who have been discriminated against decide to take revenge against those responsible in their own hands? Consider both the two sides involved and society as a whole.
- What better ways of fighting discrimination can you think of?

In this excerpt from The Merchant of Venice, *the Venetian moneylender Shylock, resentful of the numerous acts of discrimination he has had to endure as a Jew from the Christian merchant Antonio, uses his chance to take revenge. To borrow 3000 ducats, Antonio has agreed to a contract which allows Shylock to cut a pound of flesh from Antonio's body if the money is not paid back in time. Another merchant, Salerio, asks Shylock about this bond.*

SALERIO I'm sure if he forfeit you'll not take his flesh. What's that good for?

SHYLOCK To bait fish withal. If it will feed nothing else, it will feed my revenge. He hath disgraced me and hindered me half a million, laughed at my losses, mocked at my gains, scorned my nation, thwarted my bargains, cooled my friends, heated mine enemies, and what's his reason? I am a Jew! Hath not a Jew eyes? Hath not a Jew hands? Organs, dimensions? Senses, affections, passions? Fed with the same food? Hurt with the same weapons? Subject to the same diseases? Healed by the same means? Warmed and cooled by the same winter and summer as a Christian is? If you prick us, do we not bleed? If you tickle us, do we not laugh? If you poison us, do we not die? And if you wrong us, shall we not revenge? If we are like you in the rest, we will resemble you in that. If a Jew wrong a Christian, what is his humility? Revenge. If a Christian wrong a Jew, what should his sufferance be by Christian example? Why, revenge. The villainy you teach me I will execute. And it shall go hard but I will better the instruction.

From: The Merchant of Venice, *Act III, scene 1*

Comprehension

1 Complete the sentences using information from the text.
1. Shylock insists on his bond because ...
2. According to Shylock, Antonio has wronged him by ...
3. Shylock thinks Jews and Christians are ...

Analysis

2 Analyse the *rhetorical strategies Shylock uses to convince Salerio that his revenge is justified.

Annotations
- 1 **forfeit** be unable to repay
- 3 **bait fish withal** catch fish with it
- 3 **feed my revenge** keep my hunger for revenge alive
- 4 **disgraced** dishonoured, humiliated
- 4 **hindered me half a million** blocked my efforts to achieve success in life half a million times
- 5 **scorned my nation** ridiculed his Jewishness
- 6 **thwarted my bargains** interfered with my business
- 6 **cooled my friends** made my friends turn away from me
- 6 **heated mine enemies** stirred up my enemies against me
- 8 **dimensions** bodily shapes
- 9 **affections** natural instincts
- 10 **subject to sth.** exposed to sth.
- 12 **prick sb.** wound sb. lightly with a needle
- 13 **tickle sb.** make sb. laugh by touching her/him lightly
- 14 **wrong sb.** insult sb., hurt sb.
- 16 **humility** human behaviour
- 16 **what is his humility** what will his reaction be
- 17 **sufferance** punishment
- 18 **by Christian example** according to the example given by the Christians
- 18 **villainy** evil practices
- 19 **it shall go hard** it will be difficult
- 19 **I will better the instruction** I will make your teaching even more effective, outdo you

The Canton Synagogue was built in 1532 and is located in the former Jewish ghetto of Venice.

► Check

Language awareness

3 **a** Shakespeare uses a number of *ellipses (cf. ll. 8–12). Rewrite them as complete sentences.

b Read out the two versions to a partner and compare the effect. Why do you think Shakespeare uses the ellipses at this point in Shylock's speech?

Beyond the text

4 You choose Work on either task **a** or **b**.

a Discuss what aspects of Shylock's speech could make the audience feel empathy for him and what aspects may show him in a bad light.

b Do research on the excerpt's historical background. Discuss what light it throws on the status of Jews in European societies during Shakespeare's lifetime and on the discrimination against them.

5 **a** In groups, think of ways to present this speech to great dramatic effect. You may use techniques like repetition, echoing, choral speaking, etc.

b Speaking Present your version to the class.

c Viewing Find a film version of the play online. Analyse how the delivery of the speech and the use of camera shots and lighting contribute to the overall effect.

Text 7

► More info

Annotations
- 1 **may I be so converted** will I ever change like that
- 3 **oyster** *Auster;* here: sb. who shuts up in silence (very unlike Benedick)
- 5 **well** not in love
- 7 **my grace** my good opinion
- 9 **cheapen sb.** make an offer of marriage to sb.
- 10 **not I for an angel** I won't have her even if she is an angel
- 10 **of good discourse** well spoken
- 13 **arbour** shelter in a garden
- 14 **withdraw** (here) go to the back of the stage

The course of true love never did run smooth

- Think about reasons why 'the course of true love' may not always 'run smooth'.

The complications, misunderstandings and tricks that often go along with love are a frequent theme in Shakespeare's comedies especially. In this excerpt from Much Ado About Nothing, *Benedick, who has often cynically spoken against marriage, wonders whether he will fall in love like his friend Claudio did with Hero, Leonato's daughter.*

BENEDICK May I be so converted and see with these eyes? I cannot tell; I think not: I will not be sworn, but love may transform me to an oyster; but I'll take my oath on it, till he have made an oyster of me, he shall never make me such a fool. One woman is fair, yet I am well; another is wise, yet I am well; another virtuous, yet I am well; but till all graces be in one woman, one woman shall not come in my grace. Rich she shall be, that's certain; wise, or I'll none; virtuous, or I'll never cheapen her; fair, or I'll never look on her; mild, or come not near me; noble, or not I for an angel; of good discourse, an excellent musician, and her hair shall be of what colour it please God. Ha! The prince and Monsieur Love! I will hide me in the arbour.

Withdraws

Enter

BENEDICK's friends DON PEDRO and CLAUDIO, and LEONATO

DON PEDRO [...] Come hither, Leonato. What was it you told me of today, that your niece Beatrice was in love with Signior Benedick?

CLAUDIO [*quietly*] O, ay: stalk on, stalk on; the fowl sits. [*loud*] I did never think that lady would have loved any man.

LEONATO No, nor I neither; but most wonderful that she should so dote on Signior Benedick, whom she hath in all outward behaviours seemed ever to abhor.

BENEDICK Is't possible? Sits the wind in that corner?

LEONATO By my troth, my lord, I cannot tell what to think of it but that she loves him with an enraged affection: it is past the infinite of thought.

DON PEDRO Maybe she doth but counterfeit.

CLAUDIO Faith, like enough.

LEONATO O God, counterfeit! There was never counterfeit of passion came so near the life of passion as she discovers it.

DON PEDRO Why, what effects of passion shows she?

CLAUDIO [*quietly*] Bait the hook well; this fish will bite.

LEONATO What effects, my lord? She will sit you, you heard my daughter tell you how.

CLAUDIO She did, indeed.

DON PEDRO How, how, pray you? You amaze me: I would have I thought her spirit had been invincible against all assaults of affection.

LEONATO I would have sworn it had, my lord; especially against Benedick.

BENEDICK I should think this a gull, but that the white-bearded fellow speaks it: knavery cannot, sure, hide himself in such reverence.

CLAUDIO [*quietly*] He hath ta'en the infection: hold it up.

DON PEDRO Hath she made her affection known to Benedick?

LEONATO No; and swears she never will: that's her torment.

CLAUDIO 'Tis true, indeed; so your daughter says: 'Shall I,' says she, 'that have so oft encountered him with scorn, write to him that I love him?' [...] Then down upon her knees she falls, weeps, sobs, beats her heart, tears her hair, prays, curses; 'O sweet Benedick! God give me patience!'

LEONATO She doth indeed; my daughter says so: and the ecstasy hath so much overborne her that my daughter is sometime afeared she will do a desperate outrage to herself: it is very true.

DON PEDRO It were good that Benedick knew of it by some other, if she will not discover it.

CLAUDIO To what end? He would make but a sport of it and torment the poor lady worse.

DON PEDRO And he should, it were an alms to hang him. She's an excellent sweet lady; and, out of all suspicion, she is virtuous.

CLAUDIO And she is exceeding wise.

DON PEDRO In everything but in loving Benedick. [...] I pray you, tell Benedick of it, and hear what he will say.

LEONATO Were it good, think you?

Annotations

18 **stalk on, [...] the fowl sits** start hunting, the bird sits
20 **wonderful** surprising
21 **so dote on sb.** love sb. so deeply
22 **abhor sb./sth.** hate sb./sth.
23 **Sits the wind in that corner?** Can this really be true?
24 **by my troth** [trəʊθ] used to express a slight oath
25 **enraged affection** passionate love
25 **past the infinite of thought** unbelievable but true
27 **doth** does
27 **counterfeit** *(v)* pretend
28 **faith, like enough** indeed, very probable
30 **discover sth.** (here) show sth.
32 **bait sth.** place food on sth.
33 **she will sit you, you heard my daughter tell you how** Leonato has forgotten his prepared lines.
37 **invincible** too strong to be defeated
37 **assault** *(n)* attack
40 **gull** trick
41 **knavery** trickery
41 **such reverence** such a respectable old man
43 **hath ta'en the infection** is caught
43 **hold it up** continue
47 **scorn** *(n)* strong feeling that sb. is stupid
51 **ecstasy** passion, frenzy
52 **overborne** overwhelmed
53 **do a desperate outrage to sb.** kill sb.
55 **by some other** from sb. else
57 **to what end** why
57 **sport** game
59 **and he should** and if he did
59 **alms** good deed
60 **out of all suspicion** without doubt
61 **exceeding** extremely

Annotations

67 woo sb. try to persuade sb. to fall in love with you

67 bate one breath of her accustomed crossness change her usual manner of criticizing him

69 make tender of sth. show sth., express sth.

71 hath a contemptible spirit mocks everything

73 good outward happiness handsome appearance

75 wit intelligence

76 valiant brave

79 wear it out with good counsel get over it with advice from others

86 upon this after this

87 expectation judgement

89 when they hold one an opinion of another's dotage, and no such matter when both think the other one is in love, when neither of them is

91 would see would like to see

92 dumb-show scene without speech

94 conference conversation

95 sadly borne completely serious

97 requited returned in equal measure

98 censure sb. criticize sb.

101 their detractions criticism of themselves

102 put them to mending change for the better

104 reprove sth. deny sth.

105 argument proof

106 I may chance have some odd quirks and remnants of wit broken on me Maybe I will have to endure some jokes and not very witty remarks.

110 quips and sentences clever remarks and wise sayings

111 awe a man from the career of his humour bring a man to abandon his chosen path

CLAUDIO Hero thinks surely she will die; for she says she will die, if he love her not, and she will die, ere she make her love known, and she will die, if he woo her, rather than she will bate one breath of her accustomed crossness.

DON PEDRO She doth well: if she should make tender of her love, 'tis very possible he'll scorn it; for the man, as you know all, hath a contemptible spirit.

CLAUDIO He is a very proper man.

DON PEDRO He hath indeed a good outward happiness.

CLAUDIO Before God! And, in my mind, very wise.

DON PEDRO He doth indeed show some sparks that are like wit.

CLAUDIO And I take him to be valiant.

DON PEDRO [...] Well, I am sorry for your niece. Shall we go seek Benedick, and tell him of her love?

CLAUDIO Never tell him, my lord: let her wear it out with good counsel.

LEONATO Nay, that's impossible: she may wear her heart out first.

DON PEDRO Well, we will hear further of it by your daughter: let it cool the while. I love Benedick well; and I could wish he would modestly examine himself, to see how much he is unworthy so good a lady.

LEONATO My lord, will you walk? Dinner is ready.

CLAUDIO [*quietly*] If he do not dote on her upon this, I will never trust my expectation.

DON PEDRO Let there be the same net spread for her; and that must your daughter and her gentlewomen carry. The sport will be, when they hold one an opinion of another's dotage, and no such matter: that's the scene that I would see, which will be merely a dumb-show. Let us send her to call him in to dinner.

Exeunt DON PEDRO, CLAUDIO, and LEONATO

BENEDICK [*coming forward*] This can be no trick: the conference was sadly borne. They have the truth of this from Hero. They seem to pity the lady: it seems her affections have their full bent. Love me! Why, it must be requited. I hear how I am censured: they say I will bear myself proudly, if I perceive the love come from her; they say too that she will rather die than give any sign of affection. I did never think to marry: I must not seem proud: happy are they that hear their detractions and can put them to mending. They say the lady is fair; 'tis a truth, I can bear them witness; and virtuous; 'tis so, I cannot reprove it; and wise, but for loving me; by my troth, it is no addition to her wit, nor no great argument of her folly, for I will be horribly in love with her. I may chance have some odd quirks and remnants of wit broken on me, because I have railed so long against marriage: but doth not the appetite alter? A man loves the meat in his youth that he cannot endure in his age. Shall quips and sentences and these paper bullets of the brain awe a man from the career of his humour? No, the world must be peopled.

When I said I would die a bachelor, I did not think I should live till I were married. Here comes Beatrice. By this day! She's a fair lady: I do spy some marks of love in her.

Enter BEATRICE

BEATRICE Against my will I am sent to bid you come in to dinner.

BENEDICK Fair Beatrice, I thank you for your pains.

BEATRICE I took no more pains for those thanks than you take pains to thank me: if it had been painful, I would not have come.

BENEDICK You take pleasure then in the message?

BEATRICE Yea, just so much as you may take upon a knife's point and choke a daw withal. You have no stomach, signior: fare you well.

Exit

BENEDICK Ha! 'Against my will I am sent to bid you come in to dinner;' there's a double meaning in that. 'I took no more pains for those thanks than you took pains to thank me.' That's as much as to say, any pains that I take for you is as easy as thanks. If I do not take pity of her, I am a villain.

Exit

From: Much Ado About Nothing, *Act II, scene 3*

Annotations

123 **choke a daw withal** make a jackdaw (*Dohle*) stop breathing with it

123 **have no stomach** not be hungry

Comprehension

1 a State the qualities Benedick is looking for in a woman he might marry.

b Sum up how Beatrice's supposed love for Benedick manifests itself and why she cannot tell him about it.

c Outline how Benedick's attitude towards marriage changes during the course of the scene.

Analysis

2 Analyse how Don Pedro, Claudio and Leonato convince Benedick that Beatrice is in love with him.

3 Examine how Shakespeare achieves a humorous effect in this scene.

Language awareness

4 a Collect words and phrases in the text that describe the feelings of somebody who is in love.

b Which of them could still be used today? Which would seem odd today?

Beyond the text

5 Describe the concepts of masculinity and femininity that underlie the *protagonists' actions in the text. Comment on them and compare them to how relationships are formed today.

► Support p. 30

▶ SF 36: Creative writing, Student's book p. 311

6 Writing Imagine Beatrice and Benedick were alive today. Write a chat between them in which they try to find out if the other one wants to go on a date with them. You may also include messages between them and other characters.

Text 8

▶ Getting started

Adapting Shakespeare

- Think about possible reasons for a writer or a film director to make a modern adaptation of a text written centuries ago.

In this excerpt from Much Ado About Nothing, *Beatrice and Benedick, wearing masks and costumes, dance with each other during a festivity. Beatrice pretends not to recognize Benedick, who assumes that she really cannot see through his disguise.*

BEATRICE I am sure you know him well enough.
BENEDICK Not I, believe me.
BEATRICE Did he never make you laugh?
BENEDICK I pray you, what is he?
BEATRICE Why, he is the prince's jester: a very dull fool; only his gift is in devising impossible slanders: none but libertines delight in him; and the commendation is not in his wit, but in his villainy; for he both pleases men and angers them, and then they laugh at him and beat him. I am sure he is in the fleet: I would he had boarded me.
BENEDICK When I know the gentleman, I'll tell him what you say.
BEATRICE Do, do: he'll but break a comparison or two on me; which, peradventure not marked or not laughed at, strikes him into melancholy; and then there's a partridge wing saved, for the fool will eat no supper that night. We must follow the leaders.

From: William Shakespeare, Much Ado About Nothing, *Act II, scene 1*

Annotations
1 **him** Benedick
4 **what is he** who is he
5 **jester** *(an insult here)* Hofnarr
5 **only his gift** his only talent
6 **devise sth.** invent sth.
6 **slanders** false statements made to harm sb.'s reputation
6 **libertines** [ˈlɪbətiːnz] good-for-nothings
6 **delight in sb.** find sb. enjoyable
7 **commendation** praise
8 **villainy** offensiveness
8 **angers them** e.g. when he makes jokes which insult them
9 **fleet** company
10 **I would** I wish
10 **had boarded me** had asked me to dance with him
12 **break a comparison on sb.** make clever remarks about sb.
13 **peradventure** perhaps
13 **mark sth.** pay attention to sth.
14 **a partridge wing** a small amount
16 **leaders** (here) those leading the dance

Partner B: Read the text on p. 30 and work on the tasks there.
Partner A: Read the text below and work on task **1**.

In Lily Anderson's adaptation of Shakespeare's comedy, The Only Thing Worse Than Me Is You *(2016), the *protagonists go to a private school. In this excerpt, they meet in a haunted house set up for Halloween.*

'Do you know Ben West, homicidal clown?'

He glanced down at me, the axe going limp in his hand. From the shadowy recesses of his mask, I could barely make out confused brown eyes.

'Ben West?' I repeated. 'Skinny, handlebar mustache, really lazy insults?'

The clown cocked his head and shook it side to side.

1 **homicidal clown** referring to his disguise as an evil clown with a rubber axe
2 **recess** part that is set further back
4 **handlebar mustache** line of hair on the upper lip

'Lucky you,' I said, shivering closer to him. 'You must be new. He's less of a class clown – no offence – and more of our token idiot savant. I don't know how Cornell and Peter are putting up with his jackassery. Two minutes with West is like one really obnoxious lifetime. They'll realize it eventually. Everyone does. I mean, what kind of loser do you have to be to get kicked out of the role-playing club?'

The clown yanked the elbow I was holding onto, steering me around a group heading into the next room and toward the opposite wall. He drew back a sheet of plastic – which looked no different from the rest of the black plastic – to reveal a door that opened onto the quad.

From: Lily Anderson, The Only Thing Worse Than Me Is You, *2016*

Annotations

6 **shiver** *(v)* shake slightly
7 **no offence** this is not meant as an insult
7 **token** only pretending
7 **idiot savant** [ˌɪdiəʊ sæˈvɒ̃] sb. with learning difficulties who is unusually talented in a specific field
7 **Cornell and Peter** Claudio and Don Pedro in Shakespeare's play
8 **jackassery** *(infml)* stupidity
9 **obnoxious** extremely unpleasant
9 **eventually** in the end
11 **yank sb./sth.** suddenly pull sb./sth. hard
14 **quad** (quadrangle) open square area with buildings all around it

Comprehension

1 **a** Together with your partner, summarize what happens in Shakespeare's scene.
b Point out for your partner which elements of the original have been kept in Lily Anderson's version and what has been changed.
c Listen to your partner tell you which elements of the original have been kept in McKelle George's version and what has been changed.

Analysis

2 Compare the ways in which Shakespeare and the modern adaptation you worked on build up the tension between the two characters.

3 Work on either task **a** or **b**.
a Compare the ways Beatrice insults Benedick in Shakespeare's text and in the modern version you worked on and explain why their remarks are so hurtful.
b Challenge Compare the ways Beatrice insults Benedick in Shakespeare's text and in the modern version you worked on and explain why their remarks are so hurtful. Explain what her insults may tell us about her feelings towards Benedick.

Language awareness

4 **a** Find typical features of spoken language in the modern adaptation you worked on.
b Point out which elements should not be used in a formal text type and find suitable replacements for them.

► More language

Beyond the text

5 The numerous modern adaptations of Shakespeare show that there is a lot in his texts that still speaks to us. Think back to this chapter's guiding question and discuss what aspects of the original scene between Beatrice and Benedick we can still relate to.

Art in Context: Portraying Shakespeare

► More info

- *Quick write: Based on the texts you have read, what kind of person do you imagine the historical Shakespeare might have been? Write a short paragraph.

The Chandos portrait of Shakespeare was painted between 1600 and 1610, i.e. during his lifetime.

U.S. artist Mathew McFarren painted his 'Tattooed Shakespeare' in 2003.

Comprehension

► Getting started

1 Describe McFarren's portrait 'Tattooed Shakespeare' (2003).

Language help

In the foreground/background/middle/centre/... • be shown/depicted ... • His body language suggests ... • be characterized as someone who ... • common features • the most striking similarities/differences ...

Analysis

►SF 22: Analysing visuals, Student's book p. 292
►Support p. 31

2 Compare the two portraits of Shakespeare and analyse the graphical means McFarren uses to reinterpret the famous Chandos portrait.

Beyond the text

3 Interpret McFarren's painting: What does it say about Shakespeare's relevance to us today?

Shakespeare is all around us

- If the Shakespeare of Mathew McFarren's portrait (p. 24) were alive today, where would he work and what would he write?

Kae Tempest, born in 1985, is a British poet and hip-hop artist. In addition to several volumes of poetry, Tempest has also published essays, plays and a novel. In the poem 'My Shakespeare', the artist reflects on Shakespeare's place in our contemporary world.

My Shakespeare Kae Tempest

He's in every lover who ever stood alone beneath a window,
In every jealous whispered word,
In every ghost that will not rest.
He's in every father with a favourite,
Every eye that stops to linger
On what someone else has got, and starts to widen in distress.

He's in every young man that grows boastful,
Every worn out elder, drunk for days;
Muttering false prophecies and squandering their lot.
He's in every complex misunderstanding that springs up between a group of friends
And never seems to end, even when its beginnings are forgot.

He's in every girl who ever used her wits to outsmart the status quo.
He's in every vain self-admirer,
Every passionate, ambitious social climber,
He's in every misheard word that ever led to tempers fraying,
He's in every pawn that moves across the board
And still remains convinced that it's not playing.

So, you might think his words are ancient, you might think his words are dead but chances are you've quoted him directly if you've ever said, oh, it sets my teeth on edge, or there's a method in my madness or pure as the driven snow or my hair is standing on end or all that glitters is not gold or I haven't slept a wink or I wear my heart upon my sleeve or the beast with two backs or the word puking which is harder to believe or fighting fire with fire or having too much of a good thing. You see, his pen was mightier than his sword, but still his words are like blades that sing our very names when they strike. Here's the milk of human kindness, up in arms, break the ice, here's the green-eyed monster, here's discretion is the better part of valour, and now his words with their arms around each other's shoulders, swagger to the ends of their sentences, proud of everything they've done, of how his pages have lasted through the ages but how he has become a poet whose poetics have embedded themselves so firmly in the fabric of our language, it's like he's in our mouths, his words have tangled around our own and given rise to expressions so effective in expressing how we feel, we can't imagine how we'd feel without them. He's less the tights and garters, more the sons

Annotations
- 5 **linger on sth.** continue to look at sth.
- 7 **boastful** talking about yourself proudly
- 9 **mutter sth.** say sth. quietly and angrily
- 9 **squander sth.** waste sth.
- 14 **vain** overly proud
- 15 **ambitious** determined to be successful
- 16 **tempers fray** people get annoyed with each other
- 17 **pawn** *(n)* chess piece of the least value; here: people controlled by others
- 19 **ancient** very old
- 25 **blade** flat part of a sword with sharp edges
- 30 **swagger** *(v)* walk confidently
- 33 **fabric** basic structure
- 34 **tangled** twisted
- 37 **tights and garters** stockings and bands to hold them worn by men in Shakespeare's time

Annotations
39 **doomed** certain to fail
40 **tightened jaw** teeth pressed together
41 **rascal** *Schurke*
44 **inadequacy** state of not being good enough
45 **valiant** courageous, brave
45 **pitiful** deserving pity
46 **sore loser** unable to accept defeat without bitterness
47 **legacy** *Vermächtnis*

demanding answers from the absence of their fathers, the hot darkness of a doomed embrace.
He's in the laughter of the night before, the tightened jaw of the morning after,
He's in us, part and parcel of our royals and our rascals.
He's not just something boring taught in classrooms, in language that's hard to understand,
He's not just a feeling of inadequacy when you sit for an exam,
He's in every valiant woman, every pitiful villain,
Every sore loser, every great king, every fake tear,
And his legacy exists and lives on in everything he's written,
And if you listen you hear him everywhere,
He's my Shakespeare.

Comprehension

1 Work on the tasks below.
1 Name three examples where, according to Tempest's poem, we can recognize traits of Shakespeare's characters in everyday life.
2 Name three examples that show Shakespeare's enduring influence on the English language and explain what they mean.
3 Sum up what Tempest says about Shakespeare's relevance today.

Analysis

► Getting started

► SF 19: Reading and understanding poetry, Student's book p. 287

2 Analyse the *stylistic devices Tempest uses in lines 28–29, 38, 43–46.

Language awareness

3 Examine the function and effect of the repetitions Tempest uses in the text and find suitable expressions that could be used instead. How does that change the effect the poem has on the reader or the audience?

Beyond the text

4 Viewing Watch the short film *Shakespeare references in rap lyrics* and discuss whether Shakespeare can be considered a hip-hop icon.

5 According to Tempest's poem, Shakespeare's influence is still very present, even if we are not always aware of it.

You choose Taking this chapter's guiding question into consideration, work on either task **a** or **b**.

► Getting started (task b)

a Discuss what we can gain by becoming aware of Shakespeare's influence on contemporary language and culture as well as tracing it back to the original texts.

b We can still feel close to Shakespeare – but what about the other way around? If he were alive today, would he feel close to us? Would he be able to understand us? Discuss the question.

The inexhaustible genius

Ceyda Nurtsch

- In your opinion, how does reading a modern English adaptation or a German translation instead of the original text influence your understanding of Shakespeare? What could you lose or miss out on by doing so?

You are going to read an excerpt from an article by Ceyda Nurtsch in which she reports on the German Shakespeare society's 2019 annual conference on translations of Shakespeare's work.

▸ More info

Der Zeitpunkt ist bewusst gewählt: Jedes Jahr um den Geburtstag des englischen Dramatikers und Lyrikers William Shakespeare am 23. April herum veranstaltet die Shakespeare-Gesellschaft ihre Frühjahrstagung. „Shakespeare und Übersetzung" lautete das diesjährige Thema. Vom 26.–28. April widmeten sich internationale Forscher der Frage nach der Übersetzbarkeit der Werke des Dramaturgen aus Stratford-upon-Avon. [...]

Einer der Tagungsteilnehmer ist der langjährige Übersetzer, Anglist und Lyriker Klaus Reichert. „Jedes Mal, wenn ich ein Stück von Shakespeare wieder lese, entdecke ich Stellen, wo ich denke, wieso ist mir das nicht aufgefallen? Da steht ja etwas drin, das ist viel spannender als das, was ich bisher über das Stück gedacht habe." Als junger Mensch habe er immer „relativ flott" übersetzt, erzählt er. Doch im Laufe seines Lebens habe er erfahren, wie viele unterschiedliche Schichten in den Texten seien. „Sie übersetzen ja nicht Wort für Wort, sondern Sie übersetzen von einem kulturellen System in ein anderes kulturelles System." Doch wie erklärt er, dass sich Shakespeare immer wieder der Zeit anpassen lässt und so nie an Aktualität verliert? „Shakespeare ist einfach ein unerklärliches Genie gewesen, wie es vorher und nachher überhaupt keines gegeben hat", denkt Reichert. „Es hat große Dramatiker, große Dichter gegeben, aber niemanden mit dieser Unerschöpflichkeit." Und vielleicht, fügt er hinzu, liege es auch daran, dass sich der Dramaturg „nicht packen" lasse. „War er nun Anglikaner, Protestant, Puritaner oder ein verkappter Katholik?" Bei anderen Autoren sei das deutlicher zu sehen. Doch bei Shakespeare erwecke jede Figur eine neue Fragwürdigkeit. „Wenn Sie denken, Sie wissen was ist, stimmt es wieder nicht in der nächsten Szene. Das ist auch diese darstellerische Vielfalt", so Reichert. [...]

Den abschließenden Festvortrag der Tagung hält die Kultur- und Literaturwissenschaftlerin Elisabeth Bronfen. Sie widmet sich der Frage nach den Einflüssen Shakespeares in gegenwärtigen TV-Produktionen. In *Westworld* mit Anthony Hopkins in der Hauptrolle etwa zitiert ein Android immer, wenn er eine Störung erfährt, Shakespeare. „Man nennt das ‚Quotable Shakespeare'", erklärt Bronfen. „Durch die Shakespeare-Zitate verleiht man der Serie Autorität. Man zeigt, man ist kulturell wertvoll, man schafft eine Art Gemeinschaft, weil alle Leute diese Zitate auch erkennen." Der Einfluss zeige sich aber auch in Serien wie *House of Cards* oder *Homeland*. Die derzeitige Politik, insbesondere die US-amerikanische Politik, erinnere sehr an die Politik, die in den Shakespeare-Historien wie *Macbeth* durchgespielt werde, denkt Bronfen. „Es geht immer um blutige Machtkämpfe, um Intrigen und Zwist im Inneren.“ Und da liege es auf der Hand, die blutigen Hände der Politik in Washington und somit *House of Cards* mit den blutigen Händen Macbeths und seiner Lady zu verknüpfen. Und Bronfen fasst zusammen: „Der Geist Shakespeares geistert also weiter herum, weil er so greifbar und wandelbar ist. Und zwar sowohl von der Sprache her als auch von den Figurenkonstellationen, Geschichten und Themen, die verhandelt werden.“

From: 'Shakespeare: aktuell und unerschöpflich'. Dr. Ceyda Nurtsch, Deutsche Welle *29 April 2019*

► Getting started

► SF 47: Mediating, Student's book p. 332

1 **Mediating** This year, your school's annual project week will deal with the topic 'Warum sollen wir Klassiker heutzutage noch im Unterricht behandeln?'. Your class will contribute to the English department's entry focusing on Shakespeare, for which only texts written in English will be accepted. Think back to this chapter's guiding question, read the above text and write an *article summing up what Klaus Reichert and Elisabeth Bronfen say about Shakespeare's ongoing relevance.

Beyond the text

► SF 30: Writing an article, Student's book p. 304

2 **Intercultural communication** **Writing** Reichert, who has translated several works of Shakespeare into German, claims that 'Sie übersetzen von einem kulturellen System in ein anderes kulturelles System' (ll. 14–15). Write an *article for your school newspaper in which you discuss the main cultural differences between Shakespeare's world and that of young German readers, as well as strategies for bridging these cultural gaps.

Chapter task

After having been introduced to Shakespeare, his works and some of their adaptations, you will now be given a free hand in creating your own spin-off by writing a modern version of a dramatic scene that will be performed in front of the class or recorded and shown to them.

► Getting started

If you need some inspiration, you can use one of the following scenes or pick another one from Shakespeare's plays.

1 During a banquet, Macbeth is haunted by the ghost of his murdered victim. (*Macbeth,* Act III, scene 4)
2 Under a magic spell, the Fairy Queen Titania falls in love with an amateur actor transformed into a donkey by another spell. (*A Midsummer Night's Dream,* Act III, scene 1)
3 A quarrel between Tybalt, Mercutio and Romeo ends in a deadly confrontation. (*Romeo and Juliet,* Act III, scene 1)

1 Writing In groups of four to six, find and read a *plot summary of the play and then the scene itself. Write a screenplay with a modern *setting for your own adaptation with roles for every group member. Include a *character speaking in an aside, who briefly sums up the *action leading up to this moment in the play. Find suitable voice-overs, sound effects or music to support the action and the *dialogue of your *scene.

aside *(n)* remark made by a character on stage that is only to be heard by the audience, not by the other characters

2 You choose Speaking Choose one of the following modes for presenting your scene.

a Practice your dramatic reading of the screenplay several times and discuss how it can be made more convincing. Then, present it to the class.

b Record your reading of the screenplay. Make sure that the action comes across in the dialogue and that the listeners know who is speaking, e.g. by addressing the characters with their names or having the readers speak in clearly recognizable voices.

c Prepare a storyboard which includes close-ups, medium and long shots for the filming of your screenplay. Choose suitable costumes and props for your actors and practise the scene. Do not read from your script while performing.

Text 7

► p. 21

The course of true love never did run smooth

5 Support

You may consider the following aspects:

- the way relationships are formed
- the different roles men and women play in this
- the way they address each other
- the expectations they have of their future partners
- the involvement of friends and family

Text 8

► p. 22

Adapting Shakespeare

Partner B

Read the excerpt below from *Speak Easy, Speak Love*, McKelle George's 2017 adaptation of *Much Ado About Nothing*. Here, the two *protagonists, like in Shakespeare's original, are in costumes and dance with each other at a festivity.

'At first I thought you must have learned I was disdainful from someone else,' she said. 'Benedick Scott perhaps?'

'Who's that?' he asked, all innocence.

'You must know him.'

'I don't, believe me.'

'Lord Loquacious, they'd call him.' They were dancing, she realized. As long as she let him lead, she actually did all right. He was irritatingly graceful, and this, even more irritatingly, didn't surprise her.

'Describe him, won't you? Maybe I've seen him.'

She was tempted to say he was beyond description – the only truthful response that question warranted – but lurking within his request was the monster of opportunity.

'He's Prince's little pet,' she said after a pause. 'The speakeasy's mascot. Quick on his feet, entertaining and whatnot, but not much substance underneath. He wants to write, I hear, but he's too much a snob for it. The upper class think some skill they acquired in an expensive classroom can pass as art, but they haven't got anything real to say. They don't understand the world outside their social circle.'

By the time she finished, his grip was painful, but she pretended not to notice. Below the mask his mouth was a grim line.

'When I do meet this gentleman,' he said at last, 'I'll tell him what you said.'

Annotations

1 **disdainful** arrogant, looking down on others
1 **she** Beatrice
6 **loquacious** [ləˈkweɪʃəs] talking a lot
10 **be/feel tempted to do sth.** feel a wish to do sth.
10 **beyond description** impossible to describe
11 **warranted** made necessary
11 **lurk** *(v)* wait secretly
11 **his request** his asking
13 **Prince** Don Pedro in Shakespeare's play
13 **speakeasy** a place where alcohol could be bought or consumed illegally during the time of Prohibition in the USA (1920s–1930s)
16 **acquire sth.** [əˈkwaɪə(r)] gain sth., obtain sth.

'Oh, please do. He'll have a few nasty things to say about me, too, I'm sure. But we really ought to be nice. Why would he be here at all if he weren't desperately lonely?'

He practically threw her away from him, taking a step back. Beatrice had always been plagued with a mouth that was a little too big and a little too full of salt and vinegar or, most offensive of all, too full of the truth. Still, she couldn't imagine Benedick gave a hill of beans about her opinion – even if he truly believed she thought she was talking to a stranger.

'Sir, perhaps you –'

'Excuse me,' he muttered, the country accent gone, and stormed away. Beatrice watched him go, wondering if the slight twist in her stomach was, for the first time, guilt over speaking her mind.

From: McKelle George, Speak Easy, Speak Love, *2017*

Annotations
21 **nasty** very bad
24 **plagued** troubled
26 **a hill of beans** *(AE)* a very small amount
29 **mutter sth.** say sth. quietly and angrily
30 **slight twist** small sudden turn

1 **a** Together with your partner, summarize what happens in Shakespeare's scene.
b Point out for your partner which elements of the original have been kept in McKelle George's version and what has been changed.
c Listen to your partner tell you which elements of the original have been kept in Lily Anderson's version and what has been changed.

Now go back to page 23 and work on task **2**.

Text 9

Art in Context: Portraying Shakespeare

► p. 24

2 Support

To structure your observations, the following table may be helpful:

	Chandos	McFarren
Head and body		
Clothing		
Posture		
Background		

Acknowledgements

Cover
stock.adobe.com/Pawel

Photos
p. 4 Shakespeare: Shutterstock.com/delcarmat, point of location: Shutterstock.com/Robcartorres, envelope: Shutterstock.com/Phumsky, rose: Shutterstock.com/Sabelskaya; **p. 5** heart: Shutterstock.com/r2dpr, thistle: Shutterstock.com/Fuusen-Tango, menorah: Shutterstock.com/Erta, sword and shield: Shutterstock.com/Oleksandra Klestova; **p. 7**: Shutterstock.com/iku4; **p. 8**: akg-images/© Omikron/SCIENCE SOURCE; **p. 9**: Shutterstock.com/Meilun; **p. 11**: mauritius images/age fotostock/Classic Vision; **p. 12**: interfoto e.k./National Trust Photo Library; **p. 13**: Shutterstock.com/Phil Baker; **p. 15** top: Bill Suddick, bottom: Shutterstock.com/Plastic Ghost; **p. 16** top: Shutterstock.com/smilewithjul, bottom: Shutterstock.com/Ruslan M.; **p. 18**: Shutterstock.com/Oleg Znamenskiy; **p. 21**: Shutterstock.com/Andrekart Photography; **p. 23**: Shutterstock.com/inimalGraphic; **p. 24** left: Bridgeman Images/Taylor, John, Portrait of William Shakespeare (ca. 1610), right: Mathew McFarren; **p. 25**: Shutterstock.com/Artur Szczybylo; **p. 27**: Shutterstock.com/Tharun 15; **p. 28**: Shutterstock.com/Begin Again Studio; **p. 29**: Shutterstock.com/delcarmat

Texts
pp. 22–23: Anderson, Lily. *The Only Thing Worse Than Me Is You*. New York, St. Martin's Griffin, 2016, p. 85; **pp. 25–26:** *My Shakespeare* written by Kae Tempest. Used by permission of Lewinsohn Literary Agency Ltd.; **pp. 27–28:** "Shakespeare: aktuell und unerschöpflich". Dr. Ceyda Nurtsch, *Deutsche Welle* 29. April 2019; **pp. 30–31**: George, McKelle. *Speak Easy, Speak Love*. New York, Greenwillow Books, 2017, pp. 149–150